Garden Bugs & Insects of the
SOUTHWEST

Adventure Quick Guides

IDENTIFY POLLINATORS, PESTS, AND OTHER GARDEN VISITORS

Adventure Quick Guides

How many times have you seen a bug in your garden and wondered, "What in the world is that?" This Adventure Quick Guide provides an easy and fun way to identify common garden pollinators, pests, and aesthetically pleasing visitors. It features more than 120 insects and arthropods commonly seen in gardens of the southwestern United States.

This guide will help you learn to differentiate between pest species and beneficial insects, such as pollinators and those that can keep pests in check. The guide also includes a general introduction to basic pest control, as well as tips on how to make your garden and wider landscape a healthy, welcoming place for insects, arthropods, and other beneficial wildlife.

Cover and book design by Jonathan Norberg   Proofreader: Emily Beaumont
Edited by Brett Ortler

All images copyrighted. All photos by Jaret C. Daniels, unless otherwise noted.

Cover image: Gulf Fritillary by Bonnie Taylor Berry/Shutterstock.com

Photos identified by page in descending order a, b, c, d, e, f, g.

Michael R. Hawk: 18a
Used under license from Shutterstock.com:

Adrienne G: 4c; Akash Lanjekar: 9f; AZ Outdoor Photography: 5b; Bapi Ray: 17c; Berkeley Meyer: 22c; bobographicto: 23c; Boyce's Images: 31e; Brett Hondow: 11b, 16d; Brian Lasenby: 28a; Charles T. Peden: 14b; Colin Temple: 33b; Craig Chaddock: 18a; Creeping Things: 33d; Cristina Romero Palma: 17b, 32d; Daniel Prudek: 26b; dcb: 18d; Dennis W Donohue: 32c; Diane Isabel: 26e; D. Kucharski K. Kucharska: 34b; Elliotte Rusty Harold: 31b, 34d; Erik Agar: 20e; Ernie Cooper: 24d, 32b; Evgeniy Ayupov: 23a; Flecksy: 8e; Gerald A. DeBoer: 29a; Gerry Bishop: 16b; Glenn McCrea: 26a; grahamspics: 32f; Gualberto Becerra: 6c; Guillermo Guerao Serra: 28c; Henrik Larsson: 33c; Holly Guerrio: 13b; Ian Grainger: 18b; Ian Maton: 11d; Irfan M Nur: 24a; IrinaK: 12b, 31a; Jared Quentin: 13c; Jay Ondreicka: 13e; Jim and Lynne Weber: 5f, 7d, 29b; Joa Souza: 20d; Jody Ann: 16e; JorgeOrtiz_1976: 33a; J. T. Chapman: 5a; Jumos: 5c; KaeCsImages: 26d; kale kkm: 13d; Kamphol Phorangabpai: 17e; Keith Hider: 18c; Konjushenko Vladimir: 15a; KoreyM: 11e; Krivosheev Vitaly: grass background; Krzysztof Walasek: 15b; ktreffinger: 31c; kzww: 32e; Lam Van Linh: 19c; Leena Robinson: 4d, 9e; Luc Pouliot: 25b; Macronatura.es: 21e; Marek R. Swadzba: 16a; Maria Jeffs: 7b; Marsha Mood: 9d; Marti Bug Catcher: 34a; Marv Vandehey: 31d; Mary Allison Cowles Berg: 10c; mattckaiser: 23b; Matthew Hartshorn: 24b; Matthew L Niemiller: 6a; Mauro Rodrigues: 34c; Meister Photos: 32a; Melinda Fawver: 22b; Mirek Kijewski: 12d; msk1147: 15e; nanovector: bee icon; Nantapong Kittisubsiri: 20a; Napat: 17d; NatalieJean: 14a; natthawut ngoensanthia: 12f; Passakorn Umpornmaha: 26c; Paul Reeves Photography: 21d; Paul Sparks: 7e, 9a, 31b; Pearson Art Photo: 20b; PHOTO FUN: 15d, 29c; Protasov AN: 14e, 19a, 19d, 22d; Randy Bjorklund: 4a, 5d, 31a; Randy R: 12e; RMVera: 4b; Ron Rowan Photography: 33e; Rose Ludwig: 24c; samray: 25d; Sari ONeal: 6b, 8a, 10e, 12a; sd81: 27c; Sergio Schnitzler: 21b; Shelly Jefferson Morton: 6d; Steve Bower: 27d; Steven Fowler: 10d; Steven R Smith: 5e; Timofey Ryabkov: 29d; Tomasz Klejdysz: 14d, 19b, 22a; Tom Franks: 8c; Tyler Fox: 4e; unterwegs: fireflies background; Vinicius R. Souza: 15c, 19e; watchara panyajun: 31c; Wingman Photography: 31f; Wirestock Creators: 20c, 25a; Wollertz: 24e; xpixel: 21c

These images are used under a CCO 1.0 Universal (CCO 1.0) Public Domain Dedication license, which can be found at https://creativecommons.org/publicdomain/zero/1.0/: ALAN SCHMIERER: 7c, 8b, 11c, 16c; Robb Hannawacker: 27b

This image is used under a Public Domain Mark 1.0 license, which can be found at https://creativecommons.org/publicdomain/mark/1.0/: Dave Beaudette: 28b

These images are used under an Attribution 2.0 Generic (CC BY 2.0) license, which can be found at https://creativecommons.org/licenses/by/2.0/: Andy Reago & Chrissy McClarren: 13a, original image at https://www.flickr.com/photos/wildreturn/14144999449/; Christina Butler: 21a, original image at https://www.flickr.com/photos/144198875@N02/48720331102/; Judy Gallagher: 25c, original image at https://www.flickr.com/photos/52450054@N04/26972185476/; 27a, original image at https://www.flickr.com/photos/52450054@N04/33329599950/

This image is used under a CC Attribution 3.0 license, which can be found at https://creativecommons.org/licenses/by/3.0/us/: Whitney Cranshaw, Colorado State University, Bugwood.org: 30d, original image at https://www.insectimages.org/browse/detail.cfm?imgnum=5188038

10 9 8 7 6 5 4 3 2 1

KEY

- Species marked with this icon ⬢ are pollinators.
- Species marked with this icon **P** are pests.
- Species marked with these icons **V** or **B** are either an aesthetic garden visitor or a beneficial predator of pest species.
- Species marked with this icon **D** spread plant disease.

GARDEN BUGS OF THE SOUTHWEST

In everyday language, we commonly refer to insects, spiders, and other creepy-crawly organisms, such as centipedes, as bugs. They, or signs of their presence, are routinely encountered in gardens and yards. Within this diverse mix are a wide variety of "bad" bugs, regularly referred to as pests, and "good" bugs, called beneficials. Most garden pest species cause damage by directly feeding on plants, transmitting disease to plants in the process, or indirectly damage or disturb plants by their activities. The resulting damage can be simply aesthetic or can lead to poor plant performance, deformed growth, reduced yield, or even death. Other pests can cause damage to structures or present a nuisance by their presence. Beneficials are a gardener's best friends. They provide natural pest control by feeding on or parasitizing undesirable garden and landscape bugs, helping to keep their populations in check. Others deliver key services such as decomposition, nutrient recycling, or pollination. Many are also entertaining or attractive watchable wildlife that add to the overall enjoyment of your landscape.

Controlling Pests

It's temping to want to reach for a container of pesticide at the first sign of a pest problem. This strategy, however, can often be counterproductive. Many commonly available pesticides can be harmful to humans, other wildlife, and the environment, especially if overused or applied inappropriately. Beneficial insects, such as monarchs and bees, are particularly susceptible. Harming these "good" bugs depletes your garden's natural pest control measures.

A better and more sustainable approach is to use integrated pest management, referred to as IPM. IPM focuses on long-term prevention, not just short-term control. Monitoring is the first step. This is best done by regularly getting out into your garden or landscape and looking around. Do you see any obvious signs of pest presence or plant problems? If you do, take a closer look and try to identify the culprit. Use this guide as an aid. You can then take a sample to a local extension agent or nursery professional for confirmation. Next, it's important to assess the scope of the problem. Is it limited to a particular branch or plant, or is it impacting a larger area or number of plants? No matter what, regular monitoring is always a great strategy, as it helps you identify pest issues before they become problems. Remember, most large pest outbreaks start out small.

Now that you have identified the pest and level of infestation, you can develop a plan to control it or decide that control is not required at this particular time. IPM employs a management approach that typically involves a combination of mechanical, biological, and chemical controls to specifically target the pest.

Mechanical control can include physically removing pests from plants, using traps or barriers, or otherwise making a less suitable or desirable environment for the pest. **Biological control** uses known natural enemies against the pest. This can be a predator, parasitoid, or even a pathogen. A classic example is using ladybugs to help control aphids. **Chemical control** makes use of pesticides. Pesticides should only be used when necessary. Less-toxic alternatives such as horticultural oils or insecticidal soaps are often used first, and treatments are always applied only to the infected plant to minimize nontarget impacts. Remember, when using chemicals, always carefully follow the label directions for application rates and safety precautions.

Healthy & Diverse Landscapes

Healthy plants are more resistant to attack from pests and disease. Therefore, regular garden care and maintenance, along with a little TLC, is a great way to help prevent problems. Healthy plants also look and perform better, produce more flowers, and offer higher quality resources for pollinators.

Landscapes with higher levels of plant diversity, particularly flowering plants, tend to attract and maintain a higher abundance and wider range of beneficial insects. Collectively, such basic methods are easy to implement and offer a strong first line of defense.

BUTTERFLIES & MOTHS
Order Lepidoptera

Pipevine Swallowtail **V**
(Battus philenor)

wingspan up to 4 inches; black overall; male with iridescent blue scaling on upper side of the hindwing; female duller black with pale marginal spots; hindwing below black with blue scaling and bright orange spots; adults avidly visit flowers; larvae feed on pipevines

Anise Swallowtail  **V**
(Papilio zelicaon)

wingspan up to 3.8 inches; wings black with a broad central yellow band, marginal yellow spots and a black centered hindwing eyespot; larvae feed on sweet fennel and *Citrus*

Black Swallowtail 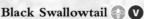 **V**
(Papilio polyxenes)

wingspan up to 4.25 inches; wings black with yellow spot band; female with reduced yellow bands and blue scaling on hindwing; hindwing with single tail; abdomen with yellow spots; larvae feed on carrot family plants, including dill, sweet fennel, and parsley

Giant Swallowtail  **V**
(Papilio cresphontes)

wingspan up to 5.8 inches; wings above dark brown with crossing yellow spot bands; wings below yellow; hindwing with single tail; tail with central yellow spot; avid flower visitor; larvae feed on *Citrus* family plants, including cultivated citrus

Giant Swallowtail Larva **V** **P**
(Papilio cresphontes)

up to 2.3 inches long; mottled brown with a cream saddle and rear end; feeds on *Citrus* family plants, including cultivated lime, orange, and lemon; can be a minor foliage pest

Western Tiger Swallowtail
(Papilio rutulus)

wingspan up to 4 inches; wings yellow with bold black stripes, a wide black margin, and a single long tail; avid flower visitor

Two-tailed Swallowtail
(Papilio multicaudata)

wingspan up to 6 inches; wings yellow with bold black stripes, black margins, and two hindwing tails; avid flower visitor

Cabbage White
(Pieris rapae)

wingspan up to 2 inches; wings white with black forewing tops and black spots; non-native

Cabbage White Larva
(Pieris rapae)

up to 1.2 inches long; green to blue-green with short hairs, a narrow yellow stripe and yellow spots; feeds on various cabbage-family vegetables, including cabbage, broccoli, cauliflower, and kale

Orange Sulphur
(Colias eurytheme)

wingspan up to 2.3 inches; wings orange with black borders in male; yellow-orange in females; some females white; hindwing below yellow with central pink-rimmed silver spot; larvae feed on clovers and alfalfa

Southern Dogface
(Zerene cesonia)

wingspan up to 3 Inches; wings yellow; forewing with pointed tip, black eyespot, and black markings outlining the silhouette of a dog's head in profile; hindwing seasonally variable from yellow to rosy-pink; larvae feed on alfalfa, prairie clovers, and false indigo

Sleepy Orange
(Abaeis nicippe)

wingspan up to 2.2 inches; wings above bright orange with irregular black margins; wings below seasonally variable from bright butter-yellow to reddish-brown; larvae feed on *Senna*; adults are avid flower visitors

Mexican Yellow
(Eurema mexicana)

wingspan up to 2.2 inches; wings above creamy white with some yellow; forewing with irregular black margins outlining a dog's head in profile; hindwings pointed on bottom; larvae feed on *Acacia* and other pea family plants

Cloudless Sulphur
(Phoebis sennae)

wingspan up to 3.25 inches; wings mostly unmarked lemon-yellow in males; lemon to pale yellow with narrow dark border and central spot on forewing in females; seasonally variable; avid flower visitor; feeds with wings closed

Cloudless Sulphur Larva
(Phoebis sennae)

up to 1.8 inches long; green to yellow with a bright yellow stripe and blue spots along the side and numerous small black spots; larvae are green if feeding on leaves, yellow if feeding on flowers; feed on various *Senna* spp.

Dainty Sulphur
(Nathalis iole)

wingspan up to 1.2 inches; wings above yellow with black forewing tip and bar along lower edge; hindwing below yellow with greenish scaling; color varies seasonally; flies low

Gray Hairstreak
(Strymon melinus)

wingspan up to 1.4 inches; wings above dark gray with orange-capped black spot on hindwing; hindwing below light gray with white-outlined black line and orange-capped black spots near single hair-like tail; avid flower visitor

Great Purple Hairstreak
(Atlides halesus)

wingspan up to 2 inches; wings above iridescent blue with black borders in males; dusty blue in females; wings below dull black; hindwing with two hair-like tails; abdomen orange-red; larvae feed on mistletoe

Leda Ministreak
(Ministrymon leda)

wingspan up to 0.9 inch; wings above brown with blue scaling on hindwing; wings below gray with thin irregular black or red and white line through center; hindwing with hairlike tail; larvae feed on mesquite

Marine Blue
(Leptotes marina)

wingspan up to 1.1 inches; wings above lavender blue in males; white and pale blue with dark borders in female; hindwing below gray-brown with white-outlined spots and bands and an orange-outlined black eyespot; larvae feed on mesquite, and other pea family plants

Ceraunus Blue
(Hemiargus ceraunus)

wingspan up to 1.1 inches; wings above blue in males; brown in females; hindwing below gray-brown with white banding and two orange-rimmed dark eyespots; forewing below with row of white-outlined black spots; larvae feed on mesquite, and other pea family plants

Reakirt's Blue **V**
(Echinargus isola)

wingspan up to 1.1 inches; wings above blue in males; brown in females; hindwing below gray-brown with white banding and two orange-rimmed dark eyespots; larvae feed on mesquite, *Plumbago,* and other pea family plants; flies low to the ground

Fatal Metalmark **V**
(Calephelis nemesis)

wingspan up to 1.1 inches; wings brown above with dark lines and a brown dark central band; forewing pointed; wings below orange with dark lines and metallic spots; larvae feed on Mule-fat and California brittlebush; adults feed and rest with wings outstretched

Gulf Fritillary **V**
(Agraulis vanillae)

wingspan up to 4 inches; elongated forewing; wings above orange with black markings; hindwing below brown with elongated silvery spots; migratory in some parts of its range; avid flower visitor

Gulf Fritillary Larva **V**
(Agraulis vanillae)

up to 2 inches long; orange with black branched spines; may have darker lines; feeds on passionflower vines

Texan Crescent **V**
(Anthanassa texana)

wingspan up to 1.8 inches; brownish-black above with white spot bands and reddish at base; hindwing below light brown with central pale band; larvae feed on various *Acanthus* plants

Bordered Patch
(Chlosyne lacinia)

wingspan up to 2 inches; wings above black with variable markings; white spots and a central orange band to narrow cream band and red markings; hindwing below black with cream band and an orange patch at the basal angle; larvae feed on daisy family plants, including sunflower, ragweed, and Indian blanket

Mourning Cloak 🆅
(Nymphalis antiopa)

wingspan up to 4 inches; wings above brownish-black with jagged margins, a broad yellow border and blue spots; wings below black with gray striations resembling bark; adults do not visit flowers but feed on tree sap and fermenting fruit; larvae feed on willows, elms, hackberries, and poplars

Monarch 🆅
(Danaus plexippus)

wingspan up to 5 inches; wings orange with black veins and borders; avid flower visitor; migratory

Monarch Larva 🆅
(Danaus plexippus)

up to 2 inches long; banded with yellow, white, and black; has two black filaments on each end; feeds on milkweeds; populations declining

Queen
(Danaus gilippus)

wingspan up to 4.5 inches; mahogany above with black borders and white forewing spots; hindwing below mahogany with black veins

Queen Larva 🆅
(Danaus gilippus)

up to 2 inches long; white with black bands marked with yellow, a yellow side stripe, and three pairs of black filaments with red bases; feeds on milkweeds

BUTTERFLIES & MOTHS
Order Lepidoptera

American Snout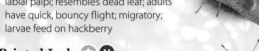
(Libytheana carinenta)

wingspan up to 2 inches; forewing with orange basal scaling and apex squared off; gets its name from long snout-like labial palpi; resembles dead leaf; adults have quick, bouncy flight; migratory; larvae feed on hackberry

Painted Lady
(Vanessa cardui)

wingspan up to 2.7 inches; wings pinkish-orange with dark marks, forewing apex black with white spots; larvae feed on mallows and thistles

West Coast Lady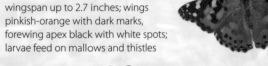
(Vanessa annabella)

wingspan up to 2.2 inches; wings orange with black markings; forewing with white spots near a squared-off tip; hindwing with a row of blue-centered eyespots; larvae feed on mallow family plants

Silver-spotted Skipper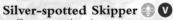
(Epargyreus clarus)

wingspan up to 2.4 inches; stout body; wings brown with a prominent white patch on the hindwing below; larvae feed on pea family plants, including *Wisteria* and false indigo bush (*Amorpha fruticosa*); larvae make leaf shelters

Funereal Duskywing
(Erynnis funeralis)

wingspan up to 1.75 inches; forewing above dark brown with lighter patch toward the apex; hindwing above dark brown with white band along the margin; hindwing below marked as above; larvae feed on various pea family plants, including deerweed, desert ironweed, and locust; larvae make leaf shelters

Common/White Checkered Skipper 🦋 Ⓥ
(Pyrgus communis/P. albescens)

wingspan up to 1.5 inches; wings black with scattered white spots; hindwing below white with tan bands; larvae feed on various mallow family plants and make leaf shelters on the host

Fiery Skipper 🦋 Ⓥ
(Hylephila phyleus)

wingspan up to 1.5 inches; wings above dark brown with orange markings in males; females with reduced orange markings; wings below yellow-orange with scattered small dark spots; short antennae; avid flower visitor; low, erratic flight; larvae feed on various lawn grasses, including St. Augustine grass but are not considered a pest

Orange Skipperling 🦋 Ⓥ
(Copaeodes aurantiaca)

wingspan up to 1.1 inches; elongated forewing; wings above orange with a little black scaling at the base; wings below unmarked light orange; short antennae; larvae feed on various grasses, including Bermudagrass

White-lined Sphinx 🦋 Ⓥ
(Hyles lineata)

wingspan up to 3.8 inches; wings and body elongated; forewing brown with cream veins and a central cream stripe; hindwing brown with central pink band; feeds like a hummingbird at flowers; larvae feed on a wide range of plants

White-lined Sphinx Larva Ⓥ Ⓟ
(Hyles lineata)

up to 3.5 inches long; highly variable in color; green with black and yellow markings and a curved horn off the rear; pupates underground; can have massive population explosions

Five–spotted Hawkmoth 🔄 V
(Manduca quinquemaculata)

wingspan up to 5.5 inches; wings elongated; forewing gray with barklike patterns, hindwing light gray with darker lines; abdomen with yellow side spots; feeds like a hummingbird; larvae feed on tomatoes, peppers, and eggplants

Five–spotted Hawkmoth Larva P
(Manduca quinquemaculata)

up to 3 inches; green with white diagonal stripes and a curved horn off the rear

Polyphemus Moth V
(Antheraea polyphemus)

wingspan up to 5.8 inches; wings tan to warm brown; hindwing with large eyespot; males with large ferny antennae; adults regularly come to artificial lights at night

Polyphemus Moth Larva V
(Antheraea polyphemus)

up to 3 inches long; bright green body with thin yellow vertical stripes and a brown head; larvae feed on various trees and shrubs

Rocky Mountain Clearwing/ Snowberry Clearwing 🔄 V
(Hemaris thetis/Hemaris diffinis)

wingspan up to 2 inches; somewhat variable in color; thorax golden; abdomen black with some gold bands; wings transparent with darker margins; resembles a bumblebee; larvae feed on honeysuckle and snowberry

Armyworm P
(Pseudaletia unipuncta)

up to 1.4 inches; variable in color; gray-green to brown with a dark stripe down the back and a pale side stripe; feed on a wide variety of vegetables, melons, and grain

Variegated Cutworm (P)
(Peridroma saucia)

up to 1.7 inches; variable in color; typically dull brown with a pale side stripe and markings; feed on various vegetables and flowers

Bagworm Moth (P)
(Thyridopteryx spp.)

up to 2 inches long; builds brown, cocoon-like structure with bits of leaves and twigs that conceal the larva inside; hangs from branches; larvae feed on various trees and shrubs; foliage pest when in large numbers

Western Tent Caterpillar (P)
(Malacosoma californicum)

up to 2 inches long; color somewhat variable; blue-gray and orange marked with black; covered in long pale hairs that are orange toward the base; feeds together in large silken webs; spring pest of various landscape trees; feed on numerous forest trees and shrubs including some fruit trees; foliage pest that causes primarily aesthetic damage in home landscapes

Cabbage Looper (P)
(Trichoplusia ni)

up to 1.5 inches long; light green with thin light stripe on the side; moves like an inchworm; pest of various vegetables and flowers, readily feeds on cabbage, kale, broccoli, cauliflower, and collards

Fall Webworm (P)
(Hyphantria cunea)

up to 1 inch long; greenish to brown body with long light hairs, broad mottled stripe, yellow spots and black bumps; head may be black or red; larvae feed together inside loose silken web on a wide variety of wild and ornamental trees; foliage pest that primarily causes aesthetic damage

Ten-lined June Beetle ⓟ
(Polyphylla decemlineata)

up to 1.25 inches long; brown oval body marked with vertical white stripes and noticeably clubbed antennae; adults attracted to artificial lights at night; larvae live in the soil and feed on plant roots; causes injury to fruit trees, vegetables, and landscape plants

Cactus Longhorn Beetle ⓟ
(Moneilema gigas)

up to 1.2 inches long; robust, shiny black oval body with long antennae marked with a white band in the center; flightless; feeds on cacti; larvae bore into stems and roots; feeding can severely harm plants, primarily attacks cholla and prickly pear

May/June Beetle ⓥ ⓟ
(Phyllophaga spp.)

up to 1 inch long; stout, unmarked shiny tan to reddish-brown oblong body; adults have clumsy flight and are readily attracted to artificial lights on spring or early summer nights; larvae live underground

May/June Beetle Larva ⓟ
(Phyllophaga spp.)

up to 1.7 inches long; white, C-shaped grubs with a dark head; live underground and feed on plant roots and decaying organic material; can damage lawns, vegetables, and flowers when in high numbers

Multicolored Asian Lady Beetle ⓟ Ⓑ
(Harmonia axyridis)

up to 0.35 inch long; oval body; pattern highly variable from unmarked orange to red with black spots; invasive; adults invade homes and other structures to overwinter; displacing native lady beetles; adults and larvae feed on other insects, including many pest species

Colorado Potato Beetle **P**
(Leptinotarsa spp.)

up to 0.4 inch long; oval, cream to tan body with black stripes and a slightly orange thorax (pronotum) marked with black; bulbous larvae are reddish marked with black spots; pest of various nightshade family plants, including potato, eggplant, and tomato

Twice-stabbed Lady Beetle **V** **B**
(Chilocorus spp.)

up to 0.2 inch long; shiny black oval body with two reddish-orange spots on the back; adults and larvae feed on other insects, including many pest species

Lady Beetle (convergent) **B**
(Hippodamia convergens)

up to 0.3 inch long; oblong body; bright orange wing cases spotted with black and a black thorax (pronotum) marked with two converging white dashes; highly beneficial predator of insect eggs and soft-bodied pests, including mites, aphids, thrips, and mealybugs

Lady Beetle Larva **B**
(Family Coccinellidae)

up to 0.25 inch long; elongated black body with orange spots; resembles a tiny alligator; highly beneficial predator of insect eggs and soft-bodied pests, including mites, aphids, thrips, and mealybugs

Seven-spotted Lady Beetle **B**
(Coccinella septempunctata)

up to 0.35 inch long; orange to reddish-orange oval body with 7 black spots and two white spots behind the head; highly beneficial predator of insect eggs and soft-bodied pests, including mites, aphids, thrips, and mealybugs

Ground Beetle ⓑ
(Pterostichus spp.)

up to 0.8 inch long; shiny black elongated oval body; wing cases heavily ridged; head with noticeable jaws; beneficial generalist predator of insects, slugs, and earthworms

Fiery Searcher ⓥ ⓑ
(Calosoma scrutator)

up to 1.3 inches long; robust body with iridescent green wing cases edged in copper or violet, a violet thorax (pronotum), and powerful jaws; quick and voracious predators of insect larvae, including many pest species

Fig Beetle ⓟ
(Cotinis mutabilis)

up to 1.3 inches long; robust green body with golden-tan edges on the wing cases; adults feed primarily on soft fruit, including grapes, tomatoes, figs, and cacti; may also feed on flowers or vegetation

Spotted Cucumber Beetle ⓟ ⓓ
(Diabrotica undecimpunctata)

up to 0.25 inch long; wing cases are yellow with black spots; adults feed on leaves, flowers, and fruit; larvae attack the roots and stems; vectors of plant disease; feeds primarily on squash, melons, and cucumber

Palo Verde Borer ⓥ ⓟ
(Derobrachus geminatus)

up to 3 inches long; elongated brown oval body; long antennae; head with noticeable jaws and may bite if handled; larvae feed on the roots of landscape trees, including Palo Verde

Vegetable Leafminer
(Liriomyza sativae)

up to 0.1 inch long; tiny; yellow and black body with transparent wings; larvae feed within leaf tissues, causing visible pale trails; feeds on wide variety of vegetables, including beans, tomatoes, melons, and peppers

Crane Fly ⓥ
(Family Tipulidae)

up to 2.5 inches long, including legs; slender body with very long, thin legs and two elongated wings; resembles a large mosquito; larvae feed on organic matter; adults are harmless and do not bite

Southern House Mosquito 🪰 ⓟ ⓓ
(Culex quinquefasciatus)

up to 0.17 inch long; narrow, striped body with two wings, long, thin legs and a prominent proboscis; females bite to collect a blood meal; considerable nuisance and occasional disease vector

Mosquito Larva ⓟ
(Family Culicidae)

up to 0.2 inch long; aquatic living near surface; elongated brown segmented body with no legs and a long breathing siphon on the rear end; often wiggles back and forth in the water

Long-legged Fly ⓥ ⓑ
(Family Dolichopodidae)

up to 0.35 inch; metallic green to copper body; bright eyes; mostly transparent wings and long, thin legs; often seen perching on leaves; adults prey on pests, including aphids, spider mites, thrips, and whiteflies

Robber Fly/Bee Killer 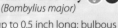 Ⓥ
(Mallophora fautrix)

up to 0.75 inch long; black-and-yellow hairy body with a tapered abdomen; large black eyes; two black wings; and long, bristly black legs; resembles a bumblebee; opportunistic predators of bees and wasps; perches on vegetation or structures and flies out to capture prey

Greater Bee Fly 🐝 Ⓥ
(Bombylius major)

up to 0.5 inch long; bulbous body with generally golden-brown hair; two clear wings edged with black, and a rigid, forward-pointing proboscis; resembles a small bumblebee; adults hover and feed at flowers; larvae are parasites of bee and wasp nests

Flower Fly 🐝 Ⓑ
(Sphaerophoria spp.)

up to 0.4 inch long; dark head and thorax; elongated yellow and black or brown-striped abdomen, two transparent wings; adults feed at flowers; larvae are predatory on aphids

House Fly Ⓟ
(Musca domestica)

up to 0.3 inch long; gray hairy body with black stripes on the thorax, two transparent wings, and red eyes; attracted to garbage, animal waste, and decaying material

Cochineal Scale ⓟ
(Dactylopius spp.)

up to 0.25 inch long; female with red body covered with white, waxy secretion; generally immobile; males have wings and long tail filaments; produces a crimson color when crushed; feeds on prickly pear cacti; can stunt growth and even cause plant death, especially in large numbers

Mealybugs ⓟ
(Pseudococcus longispinus, various)

up to 0.15 inch long; oval body with waxy white secretions often producing a spiky or cotton-like appearance; males have wings; feed on plant juices; cause leaf discoloration, distorted growth, and disease transmission; produce sugary secretions that promote sooty mold

Asian Citrus Psyllid ⓟ ⓓ
(Diaphorina citri)

up to 0.15 inch long; elongated mottled brown body and wings; wings held over the back like a tent; nymphs have yellow-orange oval bodies with white, waxy secretions produced off the rear; transmits plant diseases

Silverleaf Whiteflies ⓟ
(Bemisia tabaci, various)

up to 0.04 inch; tiny, yellow body with dark eyes and four white wings held over the back like a tent; nymphs have an oval flattened body and are wingless; feed on plat sap; pest of wide variety of vegetable and ornamental plants; secretions can lead to sooty mold on plants

Cicada Nymph Exoskeleton ⓥ
(Family Cicadidae)

up to 1 inch long; a non-living translucent stout brown papery molt with an opening down the back; typically found on tree trunks, vegetation, or even on the sides of buildings

False Chinch Bug
(Nysius raphanus)

up to 0.15 inch; gray body with membranous brown wings, the tips of which are transparent; wings fold over the back, forming an "X" shape; nymphs lack wings; pest of turfgrass, vegetables, berries, and fruit seedlings

Giant Mesquite Bug
(Thasus neocalifornicus)

up to 2 inches; adult with elongated oval gray body; legs and antennae banded with red, and wing bases with yellow veins; wingless nymphs are red with black-and-white markings; feeds on mesquite; causes little plant damage

Bordered Plant Bug
(Largus spp.)

up to 0.5 inch; adult with oval dark gray-blue to black body with orange around the edges; wingless nymphs are shiny black with a central red spot; feeds on ornamental plants and berries; generally causes little damage, but can scar fruit

Western Leaf–footed Bug
(Leptoglossus clypealis)

up to 1 inch long; brown, elongated body with a pale zigzag band across the center; long antennae, and flattened projections on the hind legs that resemble leaves; pest of many plants, including vegetables, fruits, berries, nuts, and ornamentals, especially when numerous

Tarnished Plant Bug/ Western Tarnished Plant Bug
(Lygus lineolaris /Lygus hesperus)

up to 0.25 inch; oval body marked with yellow, brown, and reddish-brown; long antennae; attacks a wide range of vegetable, fruit, and berry plants; causes blemished or malformed fruit

Harlequin Bug (P)
(Murgantia histrionica)

up to 0.4 inch long; red and black marked shield-shaped body with a black diamond on the back where the wings overlap; feeds on plant juices; attacks many vegetables and fruit trees

Green Stink Bug (P)
(Chinavia hilaris)

up to 0.75 inch long; green shield-shaped body with slightly darker diamond shape on the back where wings overlap; nymphs wingless and marked with black, orange, yellow, and white; feeds on plant juices; pest of many vegetable, fruit, and landscape plants

Brown Marmorated Stink Bug (P)
(Halyomorpha halys)

up to 0.7 inch long; brown shield-shaped body with long, banded antennae, and light and dark bands on the edge of the abdomen; wingless nymphs are gray-brown marked with red; vegetable and fruit pest; nuisance pest entering homes; invasive

Small Milkweed Bug (V) (P)
(Lygaeus kalmii)

up to 0.5 inch; elongated oval red and dark gray body with black wing tips marked with light spots; wingless nymphs orange and black; feeds on plant sap from leaves and on stems and seeds of milkweed and oleander; adults may also consume aphids and monarch eggs and young larvae

Leafhopper Assassin Bug (B)
(Zelus renardii)

up to 0.6 inch long; elongated narrow green-brown body with red-brown wing bases and long antennae; sharp beak for harpooning prey; wingless nymphs spotted with reddish-brown and black

Green Peach Aphid **P** **D**
(Myzus persicae)

up to 0.08 inch; yellow-green pear-shaped body with dark eyes; adults may be winged or not; pest of many vegetables and fruit trees; transmits plant diseases

Boxelder Bug **P**
(Boisea trivittata)

up to 0.5 inch; black oval body and long antennae; edges of wings and abdomen marked with red; nuisance pests when they occasionally enter structures in numbers to overwinter

Citrus Cicada **V**
(Diceroprocta apache)

up to 1.5 inches; black body marked with red-brown, a pale band across the thorax; transparent wings; resembles a large fly; males produce loud buzzing courtship call from trees and shrubs

THRIPS
Order Thysanoptera

Thrips **P** **D**
(Order Thysanoptera)

up to 0.08 inch; tiny elongated yellow-green bodies with pale, feathery wings; feed on plant juices; cause plant discoloration or deformation; attack many plants, including vegetables, fruit trees, berries, flowers, and ornamentals

Green Lacewing **V**
(Chrysoperla spp.)

up to 0.7 inch long; light green slender body, long antennae, golden eyes, and four transparent wings with green veins; adults feed on pollen and nectar; often attracted to artificial lights at night

Green Lacewing Larva **B**
(Chrysoperla spp.)

up to 0.5 inch long; elongated mottled brown body tapered toward the rear; large jaws; resembles a small alligator; ferocious predator of soft-bodied pests, including aphids, whiteflies, spider mites, and thrips

Ant Lion/Ant Lion Pit **V** **B**
(Family Myrmeleontidae)

inverted cone-shaped pit typically in open, sandy soil; one antlion larva is at the base of each pit; preys on ants and other small insects that fall in

Arizona Carpenter Bee
(Xylocopa californica ssp. arizonensis)

up to 1 inch long; robust black body with some bluish shine; dark wings; beneficial pollinator; constructs nest in wood and can cause structural or aesthetic damage to buildings; primarily attacks unpainted or untreated wood

Golden Paper Wasp
(Polistes aurifer)

up to 0.5 inches long; dark thorax; elongated golden abdomen marked with black; four narrow amber wings; and a distinct waist between the abdomen and thorax; social; often constructs nest on structures or in cavities; adults are predatory on other insects, including pest species; can sting

Tarantula–hawk Wasp
(Pepsis grossa or other spp.)

up to 1.75 inches long; elongated black body with bluish shine; four black or orange wings; adult visits flowers; attacks tarantulas to paralyze them and lays an egg on the bodies; not aggressive but can sting

Western Yellow Jacket
(Vespula pensylvanica)

up to 0.7 inch long; elongated black and yellow body; four amber wings; yellow-striped abdomen; colonial; constructs papery nests, often in cavities in the ground; adults are predatory on other insects, including pest species; aggressively defends nests and stings; seeks out sugary foods and can be a nuisance

Leafcutter Ant
(Acromyrmex versicolor)

up to 0.3 inch long; reddish-brown body; collects leaves and other plant parts to culture fungus in underground nests

Leafcutting Bee
(Megachile spp.)

up to 0.8 inch long; most have a stout, black body with a compact, striped abdomen; many hold wings out to the side when foraging; collect pollen on the underside of its abdomen (often resulting in a yellow belly); cuts circular pieces of leaves for nest construction; resulting holes are best sign of its presence

European Paper Wasp  **P** **B**
(Polistes dominula)

up to 0.5 inch long; elongated black body marked with yellow; four narrow amber wings; a distinct waist between the abdomen and thorax; social; invasive; often constructs nest on structures; adults are predatory on other insects, including pest species; can sting

Harvester Ant (Red Harvester Ant) **V**
(Pogonomyrmex barbatus)

up to 0.3 inch long; reddish-brown body with somewhat squarish head; collects seeds and stores them in underground nests

Thread-waisted Wasp  **B**
(Ammophila spp.)

up to 1 inch long; black head and thorax, long thin legs, four narrow dark wings, and an orange-and-black abdomen with a long, narrow waist; nests in the ground; adults are predatory on other insects, particularly larvae

Black and Yellow Mud Dauber  **P**
(Sceliphron caementarium)

up to 1 inch long; black body marked with yellow; long thin legs, four narrow dark wings, abdomen with a long, narrow waist; preys on spiders; builds nests out of mud, often on structures

Texas Striped Sweat Bee
(Agapostemon texanus)

up to 0.5 inch long; head and thorax metallic green, dark narrow wings; abdomen metallic green in females or yellow with black bands in males; avid flower visitor

Western Honey Bee
(Apis mellifera)

up to 0.75 inch long; fuzzy appearance, black eyes, four amber wings; black-and golden-orange-striped abdomen; carries pollen on back legs; produces large colonies; can aggressively defend hives; exceptional pollinator

Red Imported Fire Ant
(Solenopsis invicta)

up to 0.25 inch long; reddish-brown body with black rear end; produces large colonies; builds conspicuous mounded ground nests; stings aggressively; omnivore; invasive

Hunt's Bumblebee
(Bombus huntii)

up to 0.6 inch long; fuzzy, robust body with a black-and-yellow pattern, abdomen with reddish band in center; four black wings, carries pollen on hind legs; colonial, nests in underground cavities

Odorous House Ants
(Tapinoma sessile)

up to 0.12 inch long; tiny, dark brown to black body; can form large colonies; seek out sugary foods, considered a nuisance pest

Sonoran Bumblebee ⬡ Ⓥ
(Bombus sonorus)

up to 0.7 inches long; robust, fuzzy body; black underneath and yellow above; black band on the thorax and black abdomen tip

Morrison's Bumblebee ⬡ Ⓥ
(Bombus morrisoni)

up to 0.8 inch long; fuzzy, robust body with a black-and-yellow pattern, yellow hairs primarily on top of the body; four amber wings, carries pollen on hind legs; colonial, typically nest in underground cavities

Arizona Mantis Ⓥ Ⓑ
(Stagmomantis limbata)

up to 3 inches long; long, slender light green, gray, or brown body; triangular head; enlarged front legs for grasping prey; immatures lack wings, adults have four wings; found on vegetation; camouflaged; occasionally attracted to artificial lights at night; predatory, feeding on other insects

Carolina Mantis Ⓥ Ⓑ
(Stagmomantis carolina)

up to 2.6 inches long; long, slender green-to-brown body; triangular head; enlarged front legs for grasping prey; immatures lack wings; adults have four wings; found on vegetation; camouflaged; occasionally attracted to artificial lights at night; predatory, feeding on other insects

Northern Walking Stick
(Diapheromera femorata)

up to 3.7 inches long; elongated narrow greenish-brown-to-brown body; very long thin legs, long antennae; highly camouflaged, resembles a twig; lacks wings; feeds on shrubs and tree leaves

Western Short-Horned Walking Stick
(Parabacillus hesperus)

up to 2.4 inches long; long slender brown body, very long legs; short antennae; highly camouflaged, resembles twig; feeds on vegetation

European Earwig
(Forficula auricularia)

up to 0.55 inch long; elongated dark brown body; wingless; prominent pincers on the end of the abdomen; male's pincers are strait, female's pincers are curved; omnivorous, occasionally nibbles on plants; beneficial predator of other insects

Mormon Cricket ⓟ
(Anabrus simplex)

up to 3 inches long; highly variable in color; robust green, brown, black, or reddish body; long hind legs and antennae; females with long pointed ovipositor off the rear (to lay eggs); flightless; feeds on plants; can be serious crop pest in outbreaks

Western Horse Lubber Grasshopper ⓥ ⓟ
(Taeniopoda eques)

up to 2.75 inches long; robust shiny black body marked with yellow; long hind legs; adults with compact wings; herbivore, feeds on various plants

Field Cricket ⓥ ⓑ
(Gryllus spp.)

up to 1.2 inches long; dark brown to black with membranous wings, enlarged hind legs, long antennae, and two prominent tail filaments; omnivore; produces loud chirping calls

Greater Angle-winged Katydid ⓥ
(Microcentrum rhombifolium)

up to 2.4 inches long; green body with long hind legs; membranous green wings; long antennae; resembles a leaf, highly camouflaged; feeds on vegetation; produces loud rhythmic calls at night; often attracted to artificial lights

GRASSHOPPERS, CRICKETS, & KATYDIDS
Order Orthoptera

Jerusalem Cricket V P
(Stenopelmatus spp.)

up to 2 inches long; tawny brown head, tan legs, large hind legs; long antennae and a bulbous black-striped pale abdomen; flightless; feeds on other insects and plant roots; often attacks potatoes and carrots

Gray Bird Grasshopper P
(Schistocerca nitens)

up to 2.5 inches long; elongated mottled yellow-brown to gray body; membranous wings; short antennae; large hind legs for jumping; feeds on many ornamental plants and vegetables

COCKROACHES & TERMITES
Order Blattodea

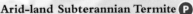

American Cockroach V P
(Periplaneta americana)

up to 2 inches long; oblong, reddish-brown body, spiny legs, and long antennae; adults have brown membranous wings; common under objects or mulch; scavengers; nocturnal

Arid-land Suberannian Termite P
(Reticulitermes tibialis)

up to 0.4 inches long; whitish to amber body with a somewhat darker head; reproducing adults have dark bodies and four transparent wings; colonial; resembles winged ant; decomposer; pest of wooden structures

Common Whitetail Ⓑ
(Plathemis lydia)

up to 2 inches long; male with stout chalky blue-white abdomen and wide central black band on wings; female with pale spotted brown abdomen and two black wing bands

Mexican Amberwing Ⓑ
(Perithemis intensa)

up to 1.5 inches long; small, yellow-brown body with orange wings

Roseate Skimmer Ⓑ
(Orthemis ferruginea)

up to 2.2 inches long; males with a lavender thorax and pink abdomen; females with white and brown thorax and orange-brown abdomen

Western Pondhawk Ⓑ
(Erythemis collocata)

up to 1.7 inches long; male with powdery blue body; females with green body; unmarked transparent wings

Twelve-spotted Skimmer Ⓑ
(Libellula pulchella)

up to 2.2 inches long; males with powdery blue abdomen; wings with 12 dark spots and 8 white spots; females with brown abdomen and no white spots on wings

Familiar Bluet Ⓑ
(Enallagma civile)

up to 1.5 inches long; slender bright blue body marked with black bands and transparent wings

Desert Firetail Ⓑ
(Telebasis salva)

up to 1.2 inches long; male bright red body with transparent wings; female dull brown with transparent wings

Carolina Wolf Spider B
(Hogna carolinensis)

up to 2 inches long; hairy gray to dark brown body with darker markings; eight long legs; resembles a small tarantula; predatory, feeds on other insects and invertebrates; nocturnal; occasionally wanders into homes

Bark Scorpion P B
(Centruroides sculpturatus)

up to 3 inches long; light brown elongated body with darker markings on the back; eight legs; pair of strong pincers off the front; curved stinger off the rear; painful sting; glows when exposed to blacklight; feeds on insects and invertebrates

Vinegaroon P B
(Order Thelyphonida)

up to 2.5 inches long; dark brown to black; six walking legs; pair of long, modified front legs resemble antennae; two enlarged front pincers; thin tail filament; feeds on other insects and arthropods

Sowbug and Pillbug B
(Order Isopoda)

up to 0.45 inch long; dark gray to brown, oval body, with plate-like segments and seven pairs of small legs; feeds on decaying plant material; found under objects, leaf litter, and mulch

Earthworm B
(Superorder Megadrilacea)

up to 8 inches or more; elongated, smooth, segmented, cylindrical red-brown to gray body; found in soil; somewhat slimy; feeds on organic material

Garden Snail B
(Cornu aspersum)

highly variable, to 4 inches long; brown to dull fleshy body with elongated stalk-like tentacles off the head; a hard shell on the back; feeds on organic material

Decollate Snail B
(Rumina decollata)

up to 1.5 inches long; cone-shaped brown shell ; brown to dull fleshy body with elongated stalk-like tentacles off the head; feeds on other snails and slugs; introduced from Europe

Milky Slug P B
(Deroceras reticulatum)

up to 2.3 inches long; elongated mottled gray to brown slimy body with a hump on the back; two stalk-like tentacles off the head; pest of vegetables, flowers, and some fruits

Harvestmen/Daddy Longlegs V B
(Order Opiliones)

up to 0.3 inch long with much longer legs; small, round, brownish body with eight thin, long legs; scavenger or predator feed on other invertebrates

Giant Redheaded Centipede B
(Class Chilopoda)

up to 8 inches long; flattened worm-like body with many legs; color variable from orange-brown body with black head and tail to black body with reddish head and amber legs; predatory, feeds on insects, lizards, and even small rodents; can bite

Yellow Garden Spider V B
(Argiope aurantia)

up to 2.5 inches long; abdomen egg-shaped with black and yellow markings; eight black legs marked with yellow or red; females much larger than males; spins large circular web with distinctive central zigzag pattern to capture prey

Banded Garden Spider
(Argiope trifasciata)

up to 0.6 inch long; bulbous black, yellow-and-white striped abdomen; eight long black-and-yellow striped legs; female much larger than male; spins large circular webs between vegetation or on structures

Two-spotted Spider Mite **P**
(Tetranychus urticae)

up to 0.03 inch long; oval yellow to orange body, with four pairs of legs; often with two visible dark side spots; resembles a tiny spider; feeds on plant sap and spins loose silk on vegetation; pest of many trees and shrubs, vegetables, and berries

Common Desert Centipede **V**
(Scolopendra polymorpha)

up to 5 inches long; color variable, brown, tan, orange to almost bluish segmented and flattened wormlike body with many paler legs that extend outward; dark bands on the back; predators of insects, lizards, amphibians, and even small rodents; can bite

Greenhouse Millipede **B**
(Oxidus gracilis)

up to 0.9 inches long; tan to dark brown or nearly black elongated, worm-like body with many small legs; feeds on organic material; harmless

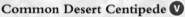

JARET C. DANIELS, Ph.D., is a professional nature photographer, author, native plant enthusiast, and entomologist at the University of Florida, specializing in insect ecology and conservation. He has authored numerous scientific papers, popular articles, and books on gardening, wildlife conservation, insects, and butterflies, including butterfly field guides for Florida, Georgia, the Carolinas, Ohio, and Michigan. Jaret currently lives in Gainesville, Florida, with his wife, Stephanie.

Adventure Quick Guides

Welcome the Guests.
Control the Pests.

**Simple and convenient—
organized by group for quick
and easy identification**

- Pocket-size format—easier than laminated foldouts
- Professional photos showing key traits
- Icons that identify pollinators and pests
- Easy-to-use information for even casual observers
- Tips to attract beneficial bugs and repel damaging ones
- Expert author is an entomologist and nature photographer

Get these *Adventure Quick Guides* for your area

GARDENING / NATURE / SOUTHWEST

ISBN 978-1-59193-981-8   **$9.95 U.S.**

PUBLICATIONS
Adventure
an imprint of AdventureKEEN